Let's COUNT Dinosaurs

© Kids Book Design Co.

HOW MANY DINOSAURS ARE THERE?

THERE ARE

9

DINOSAURS

1

2

3

4

5

6

7

8

9

COUNT THE
BLUE
DINOSAURS

THERE ARE

5 BLUE

DINOSAURS

1

2

3

4

5

HOW MANY BONES ARE THERE?

THERE ARE

6

BONES

ARE THERE MORE
EGGS OR DINOSAURS?

THERE ARE MORE EGGS

COUNT THE DINOSAURS WITH A LONG NECK

THERE ARE DINOSAURS 3 WITH A LONG NECK

1

2

3

HOW MANY
TREES
ARE THERE?

THERE ARE

7

TREES

COUNT THE ORANGE DINOSAURS

THERE ARE

4 ORANGE

DINOSAURS

1

2

3

4

HOW MANY VOLCANOS ARE THERE?

COUNT THE
DINOSAURS
WITH 2 LEGS

THERE ARE

6

DINOSAURS
WITH 2 LEGS

1
2
3
4
5
6

ARE THERE MORE PINK OR GREEN DINOSAURS?

THERE ARE MORE GREEN
DINOSAURS

HOW MANY EGGS ARE THERE?

THERE ARE

8

EGGS

1 2 3 4 5 6 7 8

COUNT THE
DINOSAURS
WITH A BEAK

THERE ARE

4

DINOSAURS WITH A BEAK

1

2

3

4

ARE THERE MORE GREEN OR PURPLE DINOSAURS?

THERE ARE MORE GREEN DINOSAURS

COUNT THE
DINOSAURS
IN THE SHELL

THERE ARE

3

DINOSAURS
IN THE SHELL

1

2

3

HOW MANY CLOUDS ARE THERE?

THERE ARE

5

CLOUDS

1

2

3

4

5

COUNT THE
FLYING
DINOSAURS

THERE ARE

6

FLYING

DINOSAURS

COUNT THE YELLOW DINOSAURS

THERE ARE

2 YELLOW

DINOSAURS

1

2

I hope you enjoyed this book!

Printed in Great Britain
by Amazon